W9-AHH-009

TEXAS TECH
RED RAIDERS

BY TOM GLAVE

SportsZone

An Imprint of Abdo Publishing
abdopublishing.com

abdopublishing.com

Published by Abdo Publishing, a division of ABDO, PO Box 398166, Minneapolis, Minnesota 55439.
Copyright © 2019 by Abdo Consulting Group, Inc. International copyrights reserved in all countries.
No part of this book may be reproduced in any form without written permission from the publisher.
SportsZone™ is a trademark and logo of Abdo Publishing.

Printed in the United States of America, North Mankato, Minnesota
052018
092018

Cover Photo: Sue Ogrocki/AP Images
Interior Photos: Sue Ogrocki/AP Images, 1; Geoffrey McAllister/Lubbock Avalanche-Journal/AP Images,
4–5, 43 (bottom left); LM Otero/AP Images, 8, 11, 31, 36–37, 38, 43 (bottom middle); Sam Grenadier/
Icon Sportswire, 12–13, 44; Karl Anderson/Icon Sportswire, 17, 43 (top); AP Images, 18; BJ/AP Images,
20; Joe Patronite/Allsport/Getty Images Sport/Getty Images, 22–23, 42 (left); Al Bello/Allsport/Getty
Images Sport/Getty Images, 25; Sean Meyers/Icon SMI/Newscom, 26; Ross D. Franklin/AP Images,
28–29, 42 (right); Joe Don Buckner/AP Images, 32; Phil Coale/AP Images, 35; Tim Sharp/AP Images, 41,
43 (bottom right)

Editor: Patrick Donnelly
Series Designer: Craig Hinton

Library of Congress Control Number: 2017962108

Publisher's Cataloging-in-Publication Data

Names: Glave, Tom, author.
Title: Texas Tech Red Raiders / by Tom Glave.
Description: Minneapolis, Minnesota : Abdo Publishing, 2019. | Series: Inside college football | Includes
    online resources and index.
Identifiers: ISBN 9781532114625 (lib.bdg.) | ISBN 9781532154454 (ebook)
Subjects: LCSH: American football--Juvenile literature. | College sports--United States--History--
    Juvenile literature. | Texas Tech University--Juvenile literature. | Football--Records--United
    States--Juvenile literature.
Classification: DDC 796.332630--dc23

TABLE OF CONTENTS

Michael Crabtree caught 19 touchdown passes in 2008.

THE CRABTREE CATCH

TEXAS TECH UNIVERSITY HAD NEVER DEFEATED A TOP-RANKED TEAM IN ITS 76 YEARS OF PLAYING COLLEGE FOOTBALL. BUT IN 2008, GRAHAM HARRELL, MICHAEL CRABTREE, AND THE RED RAIDERS' HIGH-FLYING OFFENSE SET OUT TO MAKE HISTORY AGAINST THE MIGHTY TEXAS LONGHORNS.

In 1996 Texas Tech became a founding member of the Big 12 Conference. The Red Raiders, who play in the northwest Texas town of Lubbock, had plenty of success in the new conference. They had winning records year after year. Head coach Mike Leach helped them build a reputation as a high-scoring team with a quick-strike offense.

That big offense landed them in the national spotlight during the 2008 season. The Red Raiders started the season ranked No. 12 in the preseason Associated Press (AP) poll. That ranking was due, in part, to the success of the Raiders' 2007 squad, which went 9–4 and ended the regular season with a victory over third-ranked Oklahoma. The No. 12 ranking was Texas Tech's highest in a preseason poll since 1977. The Red Raiders returned 10 players on offense, including quarterback Harrell and wide receiver Crabtree, two of the best in the country at their positions.

Texas Tech started the season with four easy wins against nonconference opponents. That bumped its ranking to No. 7 when the Big 12 Conference schedule began with the Red Raiders traveling to Kansas State. Harrell became the school's leading passer during the second quarter of that game. He broke quarterback Kliff Kingsbury's

RECORD-SETTING RAIDERS

Quarterback Graham Harrell and receiver Michael Crabtree filled the Texas Tech record book during the memorable 2008 season. Harrell set a school record with 15,793 career passing yards. He was the first player in National Collegiate Athletic Association (NCAA) history with two 5,000-yard passing seasons.

Harrell also finished his Red Raider career with a school-record 134 touchdown passes. He threw four touchdown passes in the Cotton Bowl loss to Mississippi. That made him the NCAA's leader in career touchdown passes.

Crabtree left Texas Tech after his sophomore season, but two seasons were enough for him to set records. He was the program's leader in career receiving yards with 3,127 and touchdown catches with 41—all in just 26 games.

Crabtree was the first player in NCAA history to win the Biletnikoff Award as the country's best receiver twice. He also tied an NCAA record with 13 consecutive games with at least five catches and a touchdown.

record of 12,429 career passing yards. Harrell also threw six touchdown passes in the 58–28 win.

Crabtree broke a school record a week later during a win against Nebraska. Even though he was just a sophomore, Crabtree became the school's leader in touchdown receptions with his 31st scoring catch, a 35-yard strike from Harrell in the first quarter.

The Red Raiders continued to roll, putting up a combined 106 points in victories at Texas A&M and No. 19 Kansas. Texas Tech climbed all the way to No. 6 in the AP poll, its highest ranking since 1976.

Next up was a showdown with the top-ranked Longhorns. Star quarterback Colt McCoy, wide receiver Jordan Shipley, and defensive lineman Brian Orakpo had led Texas to an 8–0 record. And the Longhorns had won five straight games and eight of their last nine against the Red Raiders. They arrived in Lubbock with all the swagger of a bully looking to squash an annoying little brother on the way to much bigger things.

November 1, 2008, was the biggest day in Texas Tech football history. ESPN broadcast its popular pregame show, *College GameDay*, live from the Lubbock campus that morning. A school-record crowd of 56,333 people showed up that night. And they were thrilled at what they saw on the field.

The Red Raiders jumped out to a big lead against the top-ranked Longhorns. On Texas's first offensive play, defensive lineman Colby Whitlock slashed through the line of scrimmage and tackled Longhorns

running back Chris Ogbonnaya in the end zone for a safety. That set the tone for a huge first half for the Red Raiders. Harrell's first touchdown pass of the game made it 19–0 in the second quarter. They led 22–6 at halftime.

But the Longhorns would not go away quietly. Shipley found the end zone on a 45-yard punt return. Then, after Tech's Daniel Charbonnet returned an interception 18 yards for a touchdown, McCoy struck back. He connected with receiver Malcolm Williams on scoring strikes of 37 and 91 yards to cut the Red Raiders' lead to 29–26. When Longhorns running back Vondrell McGee crashed the end zone from 4 yards out with 89 seconds to go, the top-ranked Longhorns had their first lead of the night at 33–32.

Texas Tech fans had experienced disappointments while facing the Longhorns before. But those previous football teams didn't have Harrell, Crabtree, and a high-octane offense on their side. Junior Jamar Wall returned the kickoff 38 yards, giving Texas Tech good field position to start the drive. Harrell completed four quick passes to move the Red Raiders to the Texas 28-yard line.

Then, disaster almost struck. With the Red Raiders fans roaring, Harrell tried to hit wide receiver Edward Britton at the 20. Britton had already caught 7 passes for 139 yards on the night. But this one bounced off his hands and popped high in the air. Four Longhorns defenders converged on the ball. Safety Blake Gideon was in position to make the interception, but the ball slipped through his hands.

Only 8 seconds remained on the clock. Texas Tech still had one time-out. The logical next step would be to throw a quick pass to pick up a few more yards, call that time-out, and set up for a potential game-winning field goal.

But Leach and the Red Raiders had other ideas. Harrell dropped back to pass. He looked to his right and saw Crabtree streaking down the sideline a step ahead of Longhorns cornerback Curtis Brown. Harrell fired a dart in that direction. Crabtree stopped his route at the 5-yard line and turned. He caught Harrell's pass and spun away from Brown and safety Earl Thomas, who converged on him as he made the catch.

THE CRABTREE CATCH

Crabtree kept his balance and ran the final 5 yards to the end zone. One second remained in the game. The Red Raiders had completed the comeback. Fans stormed the field before the Red Raiders could kick the extra point to complete the 39–33 victory. It was the first win over a No. 1 team in Texas Tech history.

Harrell finished the big game with 474 passing yards and two touchdowns. Crabtree was the hero with 12 catches for 127 yards and the game-winning touchdown.

The big win pushed the Red Raiders to the No. 2 spot in the AP poll. They extended their winning streak to 12 games with a 56–20 win over No. 8 Oklahoma State the next week. Harrell threw six touchdown passes—three of them to Crabtree—as the Red Raiders defeated a ranked opponent for the third week in a row.

DREAMING BIG

"On the sideline, I kind of dreamed that I would catch a pass and go in the end zone for a game-winning score. I do that in every game, but this time it happened. It kind of shocked me."—Texas Tech wide receiver Michael Crabtree on his game-winning reception against Texas

Texas Tech was 10–0 for the first time since 1938. The Red Raiders were in the discussion for a chance to play for the national championship. But those dreams collapsed in a 65–21 loss to fifth-ranked Oklahoma.

The Red Raiders finished up the regular season with a 35–28 win over Baylor in the season's final week. Harrell rallied the team back from a 28–14 deficit and threw the

Crabtree (5) makes the catch before running the final 5 yards to the end zone.

game-winning touchdown pass in the fourth quarter. The win earned Texas Tech a share of the Big 12 South Division title.

It was the Red Raiders' best finish since the Big 12 began play in 1996. The Red Raiders' 11 wins during the regular season set a school record. Thanks to Harrell and Crabtree, Texas Tech also set a school record for 79 touchdowns during the 2008 season.

The Red Raiders' magical season ended on a sour note. They lost to Mississippi 47–34 in the Cotton Bowl. But Harrell finished the season with 5,111 passing yards—the most in the country.

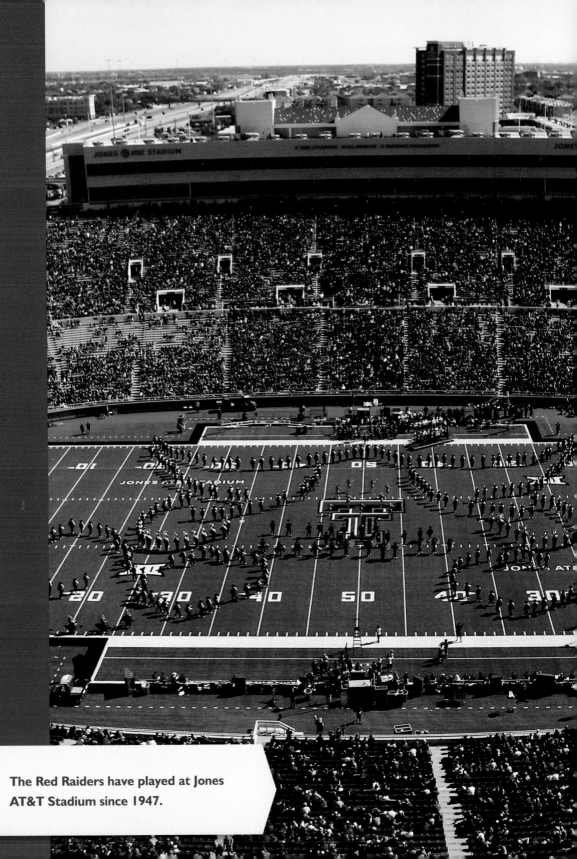

The Red Raiders have played at Jones AT&T Stadium since 1947.

TEXAS TECH FIRSTS

TEXAS TECHNOLOGICAL COLLEGE WAS FOUNDED IN 1923. E. Y. FREELAND WAS HIRED AS THE FIRST FOOTBALL COACH. TEXAS TECH'S FIRST GAME WAS A 0–0 TIE AGAINST MCMURRY UNIVERSITY ON OCTOBER 3, 1925. FREELAND'S TEAM WON ITS FIRST GAME TWO WEEKS LATER AGAINST MONTEZUMA COLLEGE AND FINISHED THE SEASON 6–1–2.

Freeland coached three more years and finished with a 21–10–6 record. Coach Pete Cawthon won 76 games in 10 years at Texas Tech. During his tenure, the school joined the Border Intercollegiate Athletic Association in 1932. Their early conference foes included Arizona, Arizona State, Northern Arizona, New Mexico, and New Mexico State.

Cawthon decided to build the school's reputation by playing a tough schedule. In the 1930s, when travel was still mostly by train, Texas Tech played all over the country, from California and Montana to Chicago and even Miami, Florida. Cawthon also chose scarlet satin uniforms that would inspire a new nickname. Collier Parrish, a sportswriter for the local newspaper, wrote after one game, "The Red Raiders from Texas Tech, terrors of the Southwest this year, swooped into New Mexico University camp today." The nickname stuck.

Texas Tech became the first college football team to fly to a road game. It took a flight to Michigan to play the University of Detroit in 1937. Texas Tech won the Border Conference title for the first time and played in its first bowl game that year. It lost the Sun Bowl to West Virginia on January 1, 1938, in El Paso, Texas.

Cawthon's Red Raiders recorded the program's only undefeated regular season in 1938. Texas Tech went 10–0 with wins against Wyoming, Montana, and New Mexico. It played in the Cotton Bowl but lost to St. Mary's of California 20–13.

Assistant coach Dell Morgan took over for Cawthon in 1941 and built a 55–40–3 record in 10 years. The Red Raiders went to three more bowl games under Morgan but lost them all—the Sun Bowl in 1941 and 1947, and the Raisin Bowl in 1949.

The Raiders' first bowl win finally came in 1952. Coach DeWitt Weaver led his first team to a 7–4 record with a 25–14 win against Pacific at the Sun Bowl. Two years later, a Weaver brainstorm gave birth to a new tradition at Texas Tech.

The 1953 Red Raiders led the country in scoring and went 10–1 during the 1953 season. They were invited to play Auburn in the Gator Bowl in Jacksonville, Florida. Weaver thought a live mascot would give his team a great lift. He recruited student Joe Kirk Fulton to create a mascot for the bowl game.

AN UNBREAKABLE RECORD

Texas Tech faced Centenary College in a heavy rainstorm on November 11, 1939, in Shreveport, Louisiana. The storm made the field muddy and sloppy and the ball slippery. Neither team could move the ball with running or passing plays.

Each team tried punting in hopes of the other team fumbling. They ended up setting a record for punts by one team and combined punts in a game. Centenary punted 38 times. Texas Tech punted 39 times. Many of the punts came on first down because they could not do anything else.

Texas Tech ran just 12 offensive plays and finished with minus-1 total yards. The teams combined for 14 fumbles. The game ended in a 0–0 tie.

Texas Tech punter Charlie Calhoun set an individual record with 36 punts, while teammate Milton Hill is in the record books with 20 punt returns on the day. The record will probably not be broken. Better fields, footballs, and equipment protect modern teams against bad weather.

In the 1954 game, Fulton burst into the stadium on a black horse. He was dressed in black with a mask and a black cowboy hat. A red cape flapped behind him. The Texas Tech players followed him onto the field. The scene shocked the crowd. "No team in any bowl game ever made a more sensational entrance," wrote reporter Ed Danforth in the *Atlanta Journal*. The Masked Rider was born.

As for the game, the Red Raiders got off to a slow start and trailed Auburn 13–7 at halftime. But the excitement soon matched the Masked Rider's initial journey earlier that day. Texas Tech took the lead when Paul Erwin hauled in a 52-yard touchdown pass from Jack Kirkpatrick. Tech's Don Lewis recovered a fumble in the end zone for a touchdown to pad the lead. Then running back Bobby Cavazos sealed the 35–13 win with two fourth-quarter touchdown runs, including one from 59 yards out. Cavazos was named the game's Most Valuable Player after running for 141 yards and three touchdowns. And in another sign of changing times, Red Raider fans didn't have to travel to Florida to catch the action. It was the first Texas Tech football game broadcast on television.

The 1953 Red Raiders won the first of three straight Border Conference titles. The 1955 championship was the last for the Red Raiders in the Border Conference. The team prepared to join the Southwest Conference (SWC). The SWC was one of college football's best. It included in-state rivals Texas, Texas A&M, Baylor, Rice, Texas Christian University (TCU), and Southern Methodist University (SMU). Texas Tech had been trying to join the prestigious conference since 1927. It finally happened in May 1956.

The Masked Rider leads the football team onto the field during home games.

Weaver's Red Raiders had losing records during the four transition years as they began adding SWC teams to their schedule. In its first season as a full conference member in 1960, Texas Tech went 3–6–1. Weaver retired after the season to enter the business world, handing the reins to assistant coach J. T. King.

Texas Tech's Doug McCutchen narrowly escapes a Georgia Tech defender to score a touchdown in the 1970 Sun Bowl.

Over the next nine seasons, King led the Red Raiders to some memorable wins and took them to back-to-back bowl games. He also pioneered a technology that would become a part of every game in the future. The first game of the 1965 season featured college football's first instant replay. Texas Tech grad Robert Walker designed a video recording and playback system that allowed King and his staff to watch plays immediately after they happened. King said it was a big help to see what both teams were doing. Texas Tech won that game against Kansas 26–7. The replay system was soon banned because it gave teams too much of an advantage and was too expensive to expect every school to purchase and install one.

Two weeks after the Kansas victory, the Red Raiders knocked off rival Texas A&M with a miraculous finish. Texas Tech trailed in the final minute of play when running back Donny Anderson scored on a trick play. Jerry Shipley took a short pass and then lateraled it to Anderson, who broke free for the winning touchdown.

King left the sidelines to become the Texas Tech athletics director in 1970. His successor, Jim Carlen, was hired away from West Virginia, where he had led the Mountaineers to a 10–1 record and a Peach Bowl victory in 1969. Carlen recorded four winning seasons over the next five years. His best team was one of the most successful in the program's history. Texas Tech went 11–1 in 1973 and finished the year ranked No. 11. The Red Raiders had wins over ranked Oklahoma State and Arizona during a nine-game winning streak to finish the season. They beat No. 20 Tennessee 28–19 in the Gator Bowl for their 11th win, tied for the most in school history.

Carlen's success was a mixed blessing for Texas Tech. It caught the attention of the University of South Carolina, which hired him away from Lubbock. Carlen's final game was a 6–6 tie with Vanderbilt in the 1974 Peach Bowl. Vanderbilt's coach, former Alabama quarterback

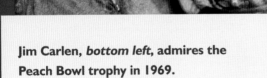

Jim Carlen, *bottom left*, admires the
Peach Bowl trophy in 1969.

Steve Sloan, had taken the Commodores to the school's first bowl
game in 19 years in just his second year as head coach. That was enough
for Texas Tech to offer Sloan the job to succeed Carlen. Sloan led the
Red Raiders to their first SWC title in 1976. The 10–2 season included

wins over rivals Texas A&M, Texas, and Baylor. After the 1977 season, he left to take the head coaching job at Mississippi.

The Red Raiders struggled for the next eight years. They had seven losing seasons between two coaches. David McWilliams started to turn things around with a 7–4 record in 1986 but left to become the head coach at the University of Texas before the end of the year. It seemed like a tough blow for Tech at the time, but McWilliams's departure opened the door for one of the Red Raiders' greatest coaches ever.

RED RAIDER RETIRED NUMBERS

Texas Tech retired the numbers of three standout players. All three are in the College Football Hall of Fame. E. J. Holub (No. 55) was a center and linebacker from 1958 to 1960. His teammates gave him the nickname "the Beast." The two-time All-American had 18 tackles and an interception return in a 1960 game against Arkansas.

Dave Parks (No. 81) was another two-way player who starred at Texas Tech from 1961 to 1963. Parks holds the school record with a 98-yard interception return against Colorado in 1962. He also held the most receiving records when he left Lubbock.

Running back Donny Anderson (No. 44) was a two-time All-American who played at Texas Tech from 1963 to 1965. His 90-yard touchdown run against TCU in 1964 is a school record.

Head coach Spike Dykes, *left*, led Texas Tech to bowl games in four straight years in the mid-1990s.

3

WINNING FOR SPIKE

WILLIAM "SPIKE" DYKES WAS NAMED TEXAS TECH'S DEFENSIVE COORDINATOR IN 1984. HE WAS NAMED THE HEAD COACH WHEN DAVID MCWILLIAMS LEFT FOR THE UNIVERSITY OF TEXAS IN DECEMBER 1986. TWO WEEKS LATER, THE RED RAIDERS BATTLED MISSISSIPPI IN THE INDEPENDENCE BOWL. MISSISSIPPI HIT A LONG FIELD GOAL IN THE FOURTH QUARTER TO WIN THE GAME AND SPOIL DYKES'S DEBUT.

But better times were ahead. Texas Tech went 6–4–1 in its first full season under Dykes. The Red Raiders beat rival Texas A&M for their biggest win of the season. Tyrone Thurman returned a punt for a score early against the No. 15 Aggies. Texas Tech forced three interceptions to seal the 27–21 win.

Texas Tech finished the 1989 season with Dykes's first bowl victory, a 49–20 romp over No. 20 Duke in the All-American Bowl. Senior running back James Gray scored four times that day, finishing his career with a school-record

A TEXAS SPIKE

William "Spike" Dykes spent almost his entire football career in the state of Texas. He played at Stephen F. Austin State University in Nacogdoches, Texas. He coached at eight different Texas high schools. And he was an assistant at the University of Texas for five seasons. He finally crossed state lines to spend three years as an assistant coach at New Mexico and Mississippi State.

Dykes returned to Texas to coach Midland Lee High School in 1980. He led Lee to the state championship game in 1983. He joined Texas Tech the next season as its defensive coordinator. Three years later, he was named head coach.

52 rushing touchdowns. For leading Texas Tech to a 9–3 record that year, Dykes was named the SWC Coach of the Year for the first time.

Three lean years followed before Texas Tech got back to a bowl game. It wasn't easy. The Red Raiders lost five straight games in 1993 before finishing the season with five straight wins. Texas Tech was invited to the Sun Bowl but lost to No. 19 Oklahoma. That was the first of four straight postseason trips for Dykes and the Red Raiders.

Things were looking up for Texas Tech. And college football was changing behind the scenes. Arkansas left the SWC in 1992. The conference was having trouble. Some schools did not have good attendance at games. Other schools were getting in trouble with the NCAA.

Two years later, Texas, Texas A&M, Baylor, and Texas Tech accepted an invitation to merge with the Big Eight Conference to form a new conference. The Big 12 would begin play in 1996.

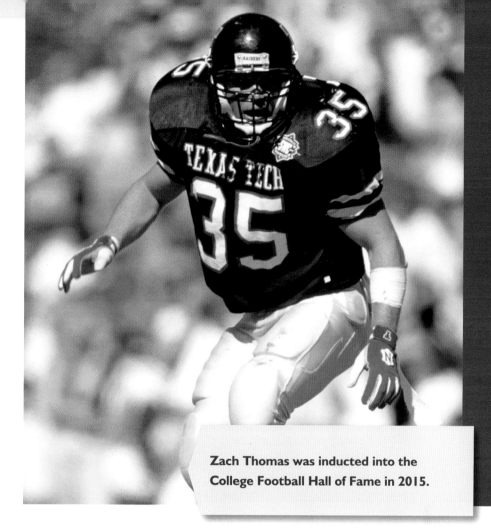

Zach Thomas was inducted into the College Football Hall of Fame in 2015.

Meanwhile the big moments kept coming. Linebacker Zach Thomas was a star, but he became a Red Raider legend with one play in 1995. The senior stepped in front of a Texas A&M pass and returned it 23 yards for a touchdown. It was the final minute of the game, and Texas Tech beat the No. 8 Aggies 14–7.

That win started a four-game winning streak for the Red Raiders. They finished the year with a 55–41 win against the Air Force Academy at the Copper Bowl in Tucson, Arizona. It was their eighth win in their final nine games. Tech running back Byron Hanspard set a Copper Bowl

Quarterback Kliff Kingsbury would rewrite the record books during his time in Lubbock.

record with 260 rushing yards and four touchdowns. Quarterback Zebbie Lethridge threw for a touchdown and ran for two more. The Red Raiders finished the season 9–3.

The new Big 12 Conference proved to be a tough challenge for the Red Raiders. But at least they were consistent. They finished with six or seven wins in each of their first six Big 12 seasons.

A special win capped the 1999 season. Dykes told his players at halftime of their final game he was going to retire. They were trailing Oklahoma 21–13. The Red Raiders wanted to give their coach one last victory. The defense forced a fumble in the third quarter, and quarterback Kliff Kingsbury scored on a short run. They went ahead minutes later when Kingsbury threw a 67-yard touchdown to Sammy Morris. Kingsbury sealed the win with another long touchdown pass.

The players carried Dykes off the field. He finished 82–67–1 in 14 years at Texas Tech. And he'd recruited Kingsbury, the quarterback of the future, who would help take Red Raider football into a new era.

HALL CALL

Five Red Raiders have been inducted into the College Football Hall of Fame. Defensive tackle Gabe Rivera and linebacker Zach Thomas join E. J. Holub, Dave Parks, and Donny Anderson among the game's best.

Rivera harassed quarterbacks for four years while playing at Texas Tech. He recorded 321 career tackles and 14 sacks. Rivera had five sacks and pressured quarterbacks 25 more times during his All-America senior season in 1982. Rivera was drafted in the first round by the Pittsburgh Steelers. His professional career ended after he was paralyzed in a car accident during his rookie season.

Thomas recorded 390 career tackles. He owns the school record with seven career fumble recoveries. He was a two-time All-American and was named the SWC Defensive Player of the Year twice. Thomas had a successful career in the National Football League (NFL). He was on the 1996 NFL All-Rookie Team and went to seven Pro Bowls.

WINNING FOR SPIKE

Mike Leach shows off the "Guns up!" salute after beating Minnesota at the 2006 Insight Bowl.

4

AIRING IT OUT

MIKE LEACH BROUGHT A NEW OFFENSE TO THE RED RAIDERS WHEN HE TOOK OVER AS HEAD COACH IN DECEMBER 1999. LEACH WAS THE OFFENSIVE COORDINATOR AT OKLAHOMA THE YEAR BEFORE. HE CALLED HIS WIDE-OPEN STYLE OF OFFENSE THE "AIR RAID," AND IT FOUND A HOME AT TEXAS TECH.

The Air Raid offense used lots of passing plays and lots of receivers. Texas Tech quarterbacks piled up huge statistics. And the Red Raiders kept winning. Leach had a winning record in each of his 10 seasons. They went to a bowl game every year. Under Leach, Texas Tech led the country in passing yards six times.

Kliff Kingsbury threw for 3,418 yards and 21 touchdowns in 2000, Leach's first season. The Red Raiders went 7–5 that year. They won their first four games but lost to the No. 1 team in the nation twice—first Nebraska, and then Oklahoma a month later.

But Kingsbury was just getting started. As a junior, he threw for 3,502 yards and 25 touchdowns and led Texas Tech to the Alamo Bowl, which they lost to Iowa. Then he put together a historic season in 2002. Kingsbury led the nation with 5,017 passing yards and 45 touchdown passes. He became the third player ever to throw for more than 5,000 yards in a season.

SPREADING THE WEALTH

"Distributing the ball to all the different skill players is our biggest emphasis. We're not a team that hands it to one guy and throws it to two. We want all five skill positions to touch the ball." —Mike Leach, talking about the Air Raid offense

Kingsbury averaged more than 50 passing attempts per game, and he put up some mind-boggling numbers in many games. At Texas A&M, the Red Raiders overcame an 18-point deficit as Kingsbury threw for 474 yards and five touchdowns, including the game-winner in overtime for a 48–47 victory.

Two weeks later, Kingsbury completed 49 of 70 passes for a career-high 510 yards in a 52–38 win over Missouri. Then he threw for 473 yards and six touchdowns in his last home game, a 42–38 win over Texas. The Red Raiders finished the year by beating Clemson in the Tangerine Bowl to post a 9–5 record. All five losses came against ranked teams.

Even after Kingsbury moved on to the NFL, the Air Raid continued. Texas Tech led the country in passing the next three years, and each year it was with a new senior quarterback who had waited his turn to

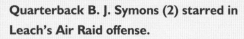

become the starter. The streak began with B. J. Symons, who broke Kingsbury's single-game school record with 586 passing yards in a loss to North Carolina State in 2003. Symons then threw for 661 yards a week later to beat Mississippi State. He led the country with an NCAA-record 5,833 passing yards, while his 52 touchdown passes were two shy of the single-season NCAA record at the time.

The next year, Sonny Crumbie led the country with 4,742 passing yards while the Red Raiders went 8–4 and won the Holiday Bowl. The Holiday Bowl win came against a No. 4 California team quarterbacked

AIRING IT OUT

Graham Harrell proved to be a perfect fit for Leach's offense at Texas Tech.

by future Green Bay Packers star Aaron Rodgers. Crumbie threw for a career-high 520 yards and three touchdowns in the 45–31 upset.

Texas Tech's success was getting noticed. The Red Raiders started the 2005 season ranked No. 21 and climbed to No. 10 with a 6–0 start. Quarterback Cody Hodges threw for 643 yards against Kansas State in the sixth victory. Joel Filani set a Big 12 record with 255 receiving yards in that victory. The great start was spoiled by a 52–17 loss to No. 2 Texas, who would go on to win the national title that year. Tech finished the regular season with a big win against Oklahoma. Running back Taurean Henderson slipped into the end zone on the final play of the game. Referees had to go to replay to see if he had scored. The touchdown stood, and the Red Raiders won 23–21. The win sent them to the Cotton Bowl, where they lost a heart-breaker to Alabama 13–10 on a late field goal.

The next year, for the first time in four seasons, Leach didn't hand the reins to a senior quarterback. Sophomore Graham Harrell was in charge of the Air Raid, and he became the next great Texas Tech quarterback. Harrell led the country in pass attempts and completions and was second in touchdowns in 2006. The Red Raiders went 7–5 and were invited to the Insight Bowl, where they made more history.

Texas Tech trailed Minnesota 35–7 at halftime of the bowl game. The Golden Gophers added a field goal midway through the third quarter and led 38–7. Then the Red Raiders rallied. Harrell threw a 43-yard touchdown pass to Filani to get the comeback started. He then hit Robert Johnson for an 8-yard score early in the fourth quarter to get within 38–21. The Red Raiders' quick-strike offense set up short touchdown runs by Harrell and Shannon Woods to get within 38–35 with 2:39 left. Alex Trlica then nailed a 52-yard field goal as time expired to tie the game.

Minnesota kicked a field goal to start overtime, but Tech won it on Woods's 3-yard touchdown run. Harrell finished the game with 445 passing yards. It was the largest comeback in bowl history.

Texas Tech led the country in passing again in 2007 and 2008 as Harrell and Michael Crabtree put the Red Raiders on the national map.

They finished the 2007 season beating No. 3 Oklahoma, thanks in part to 420 passing yards from Harrell. Then he threw for 407 yards to lead a comeback in the Gator Bowl against No. 21 Virginia.

Harrell finished the season with 5,705 passing yards, trailing only Symons's NCAA-record season. Crabtree set NCAA freshman records with 134 receptions, 1,962 yards, and 22 touchdowns.

Harrell and Crabtree returned for Tech's magical 2008 season. After wins against No. 19 Kansas, No. 1 Texas, and No. 8 Oklahoma State, the Red Raiders were ranked No. 2 in the country. They were in the hunt for a national championship. But it didn't work out. And a year later, Leach was gone. The Red Raiders went 8–4 and were picked for

INSIGHTFUL COMEBACK

Texas Tech's comeback against Minnesota in the 2006 Insight Bowl is the largest comeback in bowl history. The game is also in the record books for other reasons.

Texas Tech kicker Alex Trlica set the NCAA record for extra points without a miss. He made his 162nd straight extra point kick in the first quarter. He finished his career a year later never having missed an extra point in 233 attempts. At the beginning of 2018, that was still an NCAA record.

Joel Filani's long touchdown catch started the comeback. He finished the game with 11 catches for 162 yards. Both are Red Raider records in a bowl game. Filani's big game also put him on top of the Texas Tech single-season record charts. He finished his senior year with 13 touchdowns to tie the record. His 1,300 receiving yards that year were also a record. Both marks were surpassed by Michael Crabtree one year later.

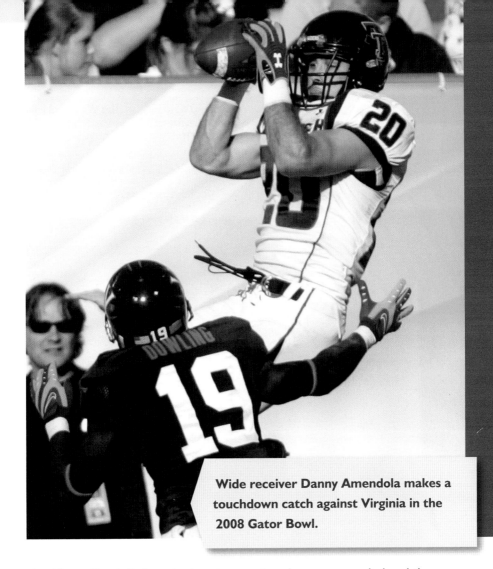

Wide receiver Danny Amendola makes a touchdown catch against Virginia in the 2008 Gator Bowl.

the Alamo Bowl. Before the bowl game, Leach was suspended and then fired by Texas Tech. The administration said Leach had treated an injured player unfairly.

Assistant coach Ruffin McNeill coached Texas Tech to a win over Michigan State at the Alamo Bowl. Backup quarterback Steven Sheffield threw a late touchdown pass to help the Red Raiders rally for a 41–31 win. Texas Tech supporters hoped the success would continue under a new administration.

Kliff Kingsbury returned to his alma mater to take over the program in 2012.

5

KINGSBURY RETURNS

TEXAS TECH HIRED VETERAN COACH TOMMY TUBERVILLE TO REPLACE MIKE LEACH IN JANUARY 2010. TUBERVILLE HAD A SUCCESSFUL RUN AT AUBURN IN THE PREVIOUS DECADE WITH ONE UNBEATEN SEASON AND EIGHT STRAIGHT BOWL APPEARANCES. TUBERVILLE ALSO FAVORED THE UP-TEMPO OFFENSE THE RED RAIDERS USED.

Tuberville had a successful first season in Lubbock, too. The Red Raiders went 8–5. Texas Tech started the next season with four straight wins. But the success did not continue. The Red Raiders won just one more game in 2011. A five-game losing streak to end the season gave Texas Tech its first losing season since 1992. It also missed a bowl for the first time in 11 years. The Red Raiders defense shouldered much of the blame. Texas Tech gave up 39.2 points per game during its season-ending losing streak.

Texas Tech returned to the top 20 midway through the 2012 season after stomping No. 5 West Virginia 49–14.

Tommy Tuberville had a 20–17 record
with Texas Tech.

Senior quarterback Seth Doege threw for 499 yards and six touchdowns
in the blowout. A week later, he threw four touchdown passes, but
Texas Tech blew a late 10-point lead and allowed TCU to force overtime.
The game ended up going to three overtimes, and Doege threw a
touchdown pass in each of them. The last one was the game-winner as
the Red Raiders pulled out a 56–53 victory. The Red Raiders improved to
6–1 but would win only one more game the rest of the way.

Tuberville surprised Texas Tech days after the regular season ended
by announcing he was leaving for the University of Cincinnati. It did not
take Texas Tech long to find its next coach. The Red Raiders hired former
quarterback Kliff Kingsbury four days later.

Kingsbury was a successful assistant at Houston and Texas A&M. He was 33 years old when his alma mater made him the youngest coach among major football programs.

Offensive line coach Chris Thomsen served as interim head coach for the Meineke Car Care Bowl. Doege rallied the Red Raiders with a late touchdown to tie the game against Minnesota. Then D. J. Johnson's interception and long return set up a game-winning field goal for Texas Tech.

Kingsbury started his coaching career in 2013 with seven straight wins. Freshman walk-on quarterback Baker Mayfield led the Red Raiders to a win against SMU in the opener. He threw for 413 yards in his first

TEXAS TECH TRADITIONS

The Saddle Tramps have led Texas Tech traditions since 1936. The all-male spirit group took its name from the term for traveling workers who spend a brief time helping at a farm before moving on.

One tradition occurs on the sidelines during games. The Saddle Tramps ring a giant bell called Bangin' Bertha to get fans excited. And they ring the Victory Bells in the Administration Building after wins.

A member of the Saddle Tramps created the mascot Raider Red in 1971. Raider Red has a bushy red mustache and a big white cowboy hat, and he fires two 12-gauge shotguns, which have shells filled with powder, into the air after touchdowns and field goals. And a Texas Tech alumnus created a hand sign to cheer for the Red Raiders. Fans point their index fingers up and their thumbs out and yell, "Guns up!"

game. When Mayfield was injured in the third game of the season, freshman Davis Webb replaced him and led the Red Raiders to a victory over No. 24 TCU. Mayfield got hurt again two games later, and Webb took over the starting job.

But the hot start did not last. The Red Raiders again lost five straight to end the regular season. Texas Tech snapped the losing streak by beating No. 16 Arizona State in the Holiday Bowl. Webb threw four touchdown passes. Jace Amaro was an All-American tight end. He had 112 yards with eight catches. He finished the season with 1,352 receiving yards, a Division I record for tight ends.

Mayfield transferred to Oklahoma, and Webb remained the starter in 2014. But the team struggled, winning just four games. Webb missed the final four games with an injury. Freshman Patrick Mahomes replaced him and provided a spark of hope in an otherwise dreary season. Mahomes set a Big 12 freshman record with 598 passing yards in the season finale against Baylor.

Mahomes carried that momentum into 2015, leading the No. 2 scoring offense in the country at 45.1 points per game. But Texas Tech went 7–6 after losing to No. 22 Louisiana State University (LSU) in the Texas Bowl. Mahomes threw for four touchdowns in the bowl loss. But the Red Raiders had trouble slowing LSU running back Leonard Fournette, who scored five touchdowns.

Mahomes came back for another season and put up huge numbers, but once again, so did the Red Raiders' opponents. Thanks to the worst

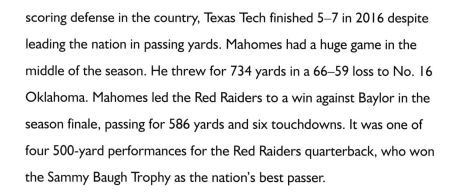

scoring defense in the country, Texas Tech finished 5–7 in 2016 despite leading the nation in passing yards. Mahomes had a huge game in the middle of the season. He threw for 734 yards in a 66–59 loss to No. 16 Oklahoma. Mahomes led the Red Raiders to a win against Baylor in the season finale, passing for 586 yards and six touchdowns. It was one of four 500-yard performances for the Red Raiders quarterback, who won the Sammy Baugh Trophy as the nation's best passer.

Mahomes left for the NFL Draft after the season. In 2017 senior Nic Shimonek threw for nearly 4,000 yards and 33 touchdowns as the Red Raiders went 6–7, losing to South Florida in the Birmingham Bowl. That left Kingsbury and Texas Tech to find the next great quarterback to lead the Red Raiders' pass-happy offense.

Texas Technological College is founded.

1923

The Texas Tech Matadors play their first football game on October 3.

1925

A newspaper writer calls the team the Red Raiders. The new nickname sticks.

1936

The Red Raiders are the first college football team to fly to a road game.

1937

Texas Tech plays in its first bowl game, losing to West Virginia in the Sun Bowl on January 1.

1938

Texas Tech leaves the Southwest Conference and joins the Big 12.

1996

Spike Dykes retires after 13 seasons as Texas Tech's head coach.

1999

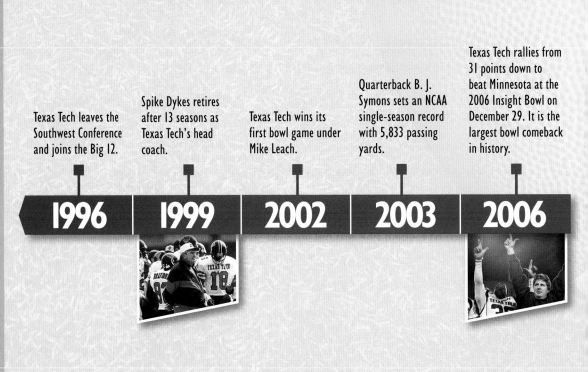

Texas Tech wins its first bowl game under Mike Leach.

2002

Quarterback B. J. Symons sets an NCAA single-season record with 5,833 passing yards.

2003

Texas Tech rallies from 31 points down to beat Minnesota at the 2006 Insight Bowl on December 29. It is the largest bowl comeback in history.

2006

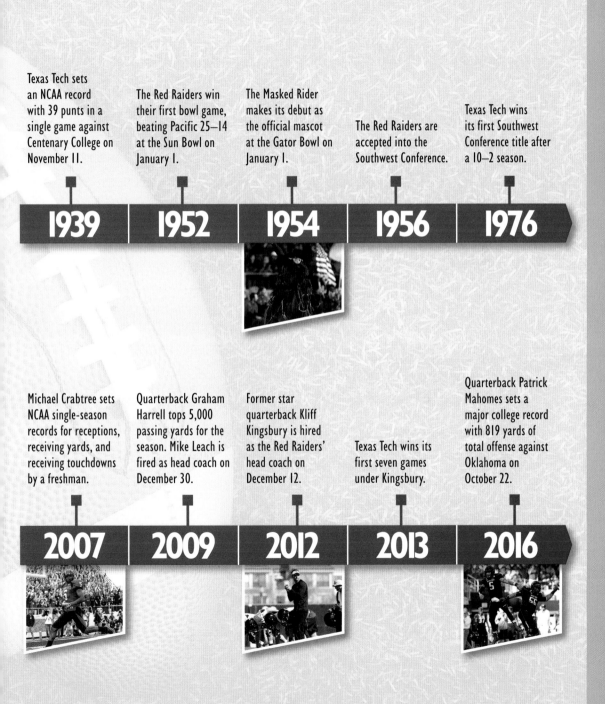

Texas Tech sets an NCAA record with 39 punts in a single game against Centenary College on November 11.

1939

The Red Raiders win their first bowl game, beating Pacific 25–14 at the Sun Bowl on January 1.

1952

The Masked Rider makes its debut as the official mascot at the Gator Bowl on January 1.

1954

The Red Raiders are accepted into the Southwest Conference.

1956

Texas Tech wins its first Southwest Conference title after a 10–2 season.

1976

Michael Crabtree sets NCAA single-season records for receptions, receiving yards, and receiving touchdowns by a freshman.

2007

Quarterback Graham Harrell tops 5,000 passing yards for the season. Mike Leach is fired as head coach on December 30.

2009

Former star quarterback Kliff Kingsbury is hired as the Red Raiders' head coach on December 12.

2012

Texas Tech wins its first seven games under Kingsbury.

2013

Quarterback Patrick Mahomes sets a major college record with 819 yards of total offense against Oklahoma on October 22.

2016

QUICK STATS

PROGRAM INFO*

Texas Technological College, 1923–1969
Texas Tech University, 1969–

OTHER ACHIEVEMENTS

Conference championships: 11
Border Intercollegiate Athletic
    Association (1932–1955): 9
Southwest Conference (1960–1995): 2
Big 12 Conference (1996–): None
Bowl record: 14–23–1

KEY PLAYERS
(POSITION, SEASONS WITH TEAM)

Donny Anderson (RB, 1963–65)
Michael Crabtree (WR, 2007–08)
Byron Hanspard (RB, 1994–96)
Graham Harrell (QB, 2005–08)
E. J. Holub (C/LB, 1958–60)
Dave Parks (WR, 1961–63)
Gabe Rivera (DT, 1979–82)
Zach Thomas (LB, 1993–95)
Wes Welker (WR, 2000–03)

KEY COACHES

E. Y. Freeland (1925–28)
    21–10–6; 0–0 (bowl games)
Pete Cawthon (1930–40)
    76–32–6; 0–2 (bowl games)
Spike Dykes (1986–99)
    82–67–1; 2–5 (bowl games)
Mike Leach (2000–09)
    84–43–0; 5–4 (bowl games)

HOME STADIUM

Jones AT&T Stadium (1947–)

*statistics through 2017 season

Texas Tech's first football game ended in a 0–0 tie. The referee ruled time had run out before Texas Tech made a 20-yard field goal. Reports later said the referee was upset he was not hired as Texas Tech's first football coach.

The Will Rogers statue was originally going to face so the famous cowboy and his horse would be riding into the sunset. But the statue's rear end would be facing downtown Lubbock. According to legend, the statue was turned so the back of the horse would be facing toward rival Texas A&M's campus instead.

"Everybody's all surprised every time this stuff happens. It surprises me everybody gets surprised, because it happens every year like this that there are surprises. The most surprising thing would be if there weren't any surprises. So therefore, in the final analysis, none of it's really that surprising."—Texas Tech coach Mike Leach in 2004 on upsets

The *Fort Worth Star-Telegram* suggested in 1925 that Texas Technical College's football team be called the Dogies. At the same time, state representative R. A. Baldwin suggested calling them the Texas Tom Cats.

GLOSSARY

alma mater
The college a person attended.

conference
A group of schools that join together to create a league for their sports teams.

coordinator
An assistant coach who is in charge of the offense or defense.

freshman
A first-year student.

fumble
To lose the ball and allow the opponent a chance to recover it.

interception
A pass intended for an offensive player that is caught by a defensive player.

lateral
A pass thrown sideways or backwards.

linebacker
A player who usually lines up behind the defensive linemen and in front of the defensive backs.

quarterback
The player who directs the offense and throws the ball.

recruit
To convince a high school player to attend a certain college, usually to play sports.

reputation
A belief held about someone or something.

sophomore
A second-year student.

tradition
A custom that is passed down.

ONLINE RESOURCES

Booklinks
NONFICTION NETWORK
FREE! ONLINE NONFICTION RESOURCES

To learn more about the Texas Tech Red Raiders, visit abdobooklinks.com. These links are routinely monitored and updated to provide the most current information available.

BOOKS

Myers, Dan. *Story of the Cotton Bowl*. Minneapolis, MN: Abdo Publishing, 2016.

Rule, Heather. *Sports' Greatest Turnarounds*. Minneapolis, MN: Abdo Publishing, 2018.

Wilner, Barry. *The Story of the College Football National Championship Game*. Minneapolis, MN: Abdo Publishing, 2016.

PLACE TO VISIT

Jones AT&T Stadium
2626 Mac Davis Lane
Lubbock, Texas 79409
806-742-3355
texastech.com/facilities/?id=2

Jones AT&T Stadium has been the Red Raiders' home stadium since 1947. It is named after former Texas Tech president Clifford B. Jones and his wife Aubrey.

INDEX

ABOUT THE AUTHOR

Tom Glave studied journalism at the University of Missouri. He has written about sports for newspapers in New Jersey, Missouri, Arkansas, and Texas. He has also written several books about sports. He looks forward to teaching his four children about many types of sports.